A MORE INTIMATE FAME.

HENRY NORMAL

INTRODUCTION

This collection is made up of the unholy trilogy upon which I've been building since I started writing poems some 5 years ago.

It is by no means a collected works as many of my other pieces are on comic or political themes that I felt were of no particular relevance to this body of material.

Since the first edition of the original booklet 'Is Love Science Fiction?' published in November 86 I've added to and amended subsequent releases.

Upgrading and balancing the subject matter, presentation and style of each, I've hopefully created a sense of progression and cohesion throughout.

With this in mind the more recent (previously unpublished) poems have been integrated into the final two sections.

And you thought it was all just flung together.

Dedicated to my mother, Joan Carroll,

ALL POEMS by HENRY NORMAL
   Flat 15, Marella Ct, 62 Delaunays Rd.
   Crumpsall, Manchester. M8 6RF
   Tel. 061 795 8684

COVER PHOTO by CAROLYN DJANOGLY

COVER SET by DAVE LEECH

PUBLISHED Aug 1990
by A TWIST IN THE TALE PUBLISHING

POEMS PREVIOUSLY PUBLISHED IN;

IS LOVE SCIENCE FICTION?
First Edition (Nov 1986)
by YOUR OWN STUFF PRESS.
Second Edition (May 1988)
Third Edition (Feb 1990)
by A TWIST IN THE TALE PUBLISHING

LOVE LIKE HELL
First Edition (Sept 1988)
Second Edition (Feb 1990)
Third Edition (Aug 1990)
by A TWIST IN THE TALE PUBLISHING

DOES INFLATION AFFECT THE EMOTIONS
First Edition (June 1989)
Second Edition (Feb 1990)
Third Edition (Aug 1990)
by A TWIST IN THE TALE PUBLISHING

LIST OF POEMS

LOVE LIKE HELL

DOES INFLATION AFFECT THE EMOTIONS?

IS LOVE SCIENCE FICTION ?

FOR YOUR ENTERTAINMENT

I will turn to channel three

And be deliriously happy
And then to channel four

I will be concerned at the future of mankind for thirty minutes or more

Then back to channel one
I will feel romance and long

For the moment when the heroine's lips touch mine

And finally if there's time
On to channel eight for some late night terror

I'll make a fatal error

Like breaking off the tuning dial
And without the presenter's soothing smile

Unable to select my channel

And without the verdict of the panel
How will I know what's real?

How will I know how to feel?

SOMEONE TOSSED A MATCH INTO THE CORNER OF OUR PAST

Someone tossed a match into a corner of our past.
It was the darkest corner
where rubbish had collected unseen.
Out of curiosity
I kindled the flame.
By its flicker I could gradually recognise
each item of debris.
Sickened with fascination
I nurtured the fervour until it blazed with fury
casting shadows onto the rest of our lives.
It raged with self destruction.
It raged with despair.
Everything and anything it could
it would drag down and wound.
Until,
wounded itself, blind and dying
strangled by its own appetite.
it shrunk and curled.
I leave the ashes now as a reminder.
I ought really to clear them away.
They seem so small reduced to cinder.
It's childish I know but
the heat has scorched so much
I have to show you before they're
finally swept

A TENDER MOMENT

I love you...........no I mean I REALLY love you.

Do you love me? Really?

Only I'm always telling you I love you but you
never say you love me only when I say it first
and then you say "I love you too" but never first.

You know it'd be nice if you said it first.
Said "I love you" without me having to say
I love you first.

No it doesn't count now.

I sometimes wonder if you really love me, you know, really.
I mean what do you love about me?

There must be something.

Don't just say you don't know.

I don't know, it doesn't count if I say it.

Oh forget it, you're bloody useless.

PREHISTORIC COURTSHIP

Menfolk tell of a fabled creature
called the female orgasm
it comes in the night
and it's so enormous
it makes your hair stand on end and your toes curl.
Menfolk enact a strange dance
to conjure up the spirit of the mythical beast
but this usually brings forth only the male of the species
which is smaller and thought to resemble a slug
due to it's sticky trail.
It is said the beast could be brought forth
if the menfolk didn't engage in the preliminary
12 pints of lager ritual

...........but that's old wives' tales.

A KIND OF LOVING

She came home one day and he'd gone
In his favourite chair he'd left a yoghurt
Unaccustomed to change
she lived with the yoghurt for three years
It never moved from the chair
They slept apart
She often wondered if there was someone else
It never ate what she served up
It ignored relatives
She would often have to hoover round it
Her sister in law told her she was barmy
to stick it out this long
But she knew that marriage was something you had to work at
She went to marriage guidance on her own
until they said they could do nothing further
if the yoghurt didn't accompany her on
the next visit
Eventually she packed her bags and left
It was a hard decision
You can't live with a yoghurt for three years
without it leaving it's mark on your life
She had some fond memories though
of those early days,
and kept a photo of the yoghurt amongst her letters.

WHEN YOUR EYES SAY "I AM HERE — IS THAT NOT ENOUGH?"

James reaches out to grasp at something tangible
He counts the number of words in your compliment
He sets every affection into an overall picture
Measures every gift against the past
If you tell him you love him he'll note it down
And consider it later
If you like a particular song he'll examine the words
For telltale signs of subconscious infidelity
If you cry he'll wonder if you're crying
For something he can't give you
In the happiest moments he steps back and looks for approval
Even with eyes caught in a tender exchange
He feels lonely
He fears one morning when nothing in particular
Seems to have happened
You'll come to him with your goodbye neatly folded
Even now your words haunt his pillow
Even now your words haunt his pillow

ANNIE

Fobbed off with crisps in a pub car park
Annie's on her own again after dark
wears what she can scrounge
earns pocket money from her paper round
for tea it's usually the chip shop
the tv and hanging round the bus stop
competes at school with the other girls
with a hungry soul from an empty world
she's not a tragic case
just another saddened face
a scruffy child trying to become a woman
feeling awkward with what she's becoming
she looks for where to cling
and finds there's something missing
clocks on at the local firm
buys going out clothes gives her hair a perm
lives for friday night
spends up out of spite

A minutes excitement is better than none
but by the morning it's all gone
still somehow she just carries on
Annie's always planning to leave
she needs time and space to breathe
still a girl trying to become a woman
feeling awkward with what she's becoming
she looks for where to cling
and finds there's something missing
at 19 Annie's married with a kid
trying to keep her panic hidden
but at last she's something clean
she's happier than she's ever been
then when he runs off to avoid ties
she sees the world in her baby's eyes
it soothes the child when they both cry
but God and only God knows why
in its sleep the baby dies
Annie looks for where to cling
and finds there's something missing

RAPE LAUGHS BEHIND EVERY SEXIST JOKE

used and abused
she lays torn
jokes about sex
aren't funny any more
her broken body soiled
by the dirt of the city
the ending is spoiled
rape scenes aren't pretty
laugh at her now and your humour's to be pitied
the scum that used her
that violated and bruised her
ripped her apart and abused her
lurks in the loudmouth on the late bus
in the drunk out to impress his mates
human skunks that reek of lust
whose words of love choke on hate
used and abused
she lays torn
jokes about sex
aren't funny any more

A HEART LIES BROKEN ON THE BATHROOM FLOOR

Why do some people shy away from mirrors
or look up into mirrors fleetingly with pain on their brow?
why do others stare at mirrors in blank disbelief
questioning, anxious, searching, longing?
why do others cling to mirrors re-checking their stance?
why do others prance like dolls
playing out their emotions and expressions before mirrors?
why do some people look long into mirrors at night
or in the quiet, praying for change, hoping to see that
which isn't there, remembering that that was,
fighting the image in the reflected mirror of their eyes?
why don't they teach you about mirrors at school?

SELF SUFFICIENT

In your dishonest silence you watch all exits
in case the logic of the big issues escape
and freedom becomes just another name for loneliness

I TURN MY BACK WHEN WE'VE MADE LOVE

I turn my back when we've made love

but not turned against you

My thoughts are of you
The curve of your body marks the horizon
The scent of you I cherish along my skin
Memories of our sex perfumes distant vales
blood has not yet settled

I've slept this way since childhood
through marriage and a dozen affairs
Unfortunately there are some things you can't un-learn
In sleep as in spirit we fall alone
Though I long to drift in endless embrace
Though open mouthed I wish for the cliche of souls entwined
This is the folly of gift shops

I will always sleep apart
Lay close
and still
We are tired as only lovers can be

LOVE — THE DISASTER MOVIE

she said she hated you / loathed you / found you utterly
repulsive / but you tried not to take it personally / now
you're standing in an empty room making a cup of tea you
don't want / and being over nice to people you hate /
measuring your success by counting the things you'll never
have / you turn on the tv to watch black and white nothing,
for a few pounds more you could have coloured nothing / you
go to the pessimists club twice a week now, it gives you
something to look forward to / you used to worry about your
lack of troubles / lying in the sun praying you didn't get
skin cancer / now you're trying to capture the world in one
sentence / dressed as lamb, you beef about the price of
love / dressed to kill you sacrifice yourself / standing in
your perfect world you look out of place / oh the words you
almost said may make you great someday / if only you knew the
rules you'd ignore them / you shrug your shoulders,
some you lose... and some you lose / there's plenty more
fish in the sea you said, but now diving in you feel like a
fish out of water and look for corners in the goldfish bowl
/ people tell you to be yourself but that's not like you /

when you're not thinking of her / you're thinking of
thinking of her / you see yourself as a prisoner trapped in
a world of reason / who's crime is that of wanting her /
who's sentence is that of loving her / and who's only
escape is to her / you're living in a world of aliens / you
feel like the skeleton in your own cupboard / like
someone's playing loud music at your funeral / it's no fun
being depressed you complain / with the ultimate vanity you
believe your inferiority complex is of a superior nature /
you believe some people wouldn't recognise love if you beat
them to a pulp with it / what did she mean we've got
nothing in common? you say / it's her, I've got plenty in
common / you wonder whether you'd rather be loved / or love
someone / or be in love, with someone you love and who
loves you / and realise you don't ask for much / you used
to be lovers / now you're just good friends / that means
she ignores you as though an embarrassment / and you watch
your words when you meet unexpectedly / I used to be
sensitive you explain / but I'm alright now, do you think?

IS LOVE SCIENCE FICTION?

"I love you" croaked the gargantuan
sprog monster from Kron 3, as it crushed
it's insignificant enemy with one claw

"I love you" sang the blue death bird
of the outer consciousness as it awoke
from a century's long sleep

"I love you" squealed the slug like bean plant
at the earth's core, as it snapped
in two to reproduce

"I love you" she said, but two weeks
later she was saying "I love you"
to someone else. What on Earth
did she mean?

TRUTH

A victim of circumstance
                from the moment of birth
no chance of understanding
                the lies you are told

A child in knowledge
                to the moment of death
how can you ever hope to know
                the truth

HOW TO BLUFF YOUR WAY THROUGH IMPOTENCE

Spending an inordinate amount of time during the foreplay engaged in providing oral sex and then being found reluctant to surface even when being dragged forcibly by the ears can easily be spotted as the first tell-tale sign there is fear of impotence. Using weight distribution and body positioning to conceal the listless nature of the reluctant appendage whilst keeping it essentially out of reach of a premature grasp by your partner is, it seems, another sure-fire giveaway.

Suggesting a cup of tea at this delicate stage may blow the whole pretence wide open. Whilst a tentative monologue along the lines of 'I think I may have a problem, it'll be alright in a minute, it's nothing to do with you, honest,' is guaranteed to sap your rapidly waning confidence.

Never accept the offer of oral sex from your partner at this juncture. The lack of even the smallest modicum of an erection is likely to ensue, resulting in egos on both sides taking an irrevocable nose dive (if you'll excuse the unfortunate imagery).

A position is often assumed at this stage with the sufferer laid poised on top of their partner some 5 or 6 inches lower than the targeted genitalia to produce a sort of carrot or sugar lump effect, which has been known on odd occasions to actually work.

This complete scenario is, of course, particularly unfortunate on a first date where no track record exists to suggest the temporary nature of the affliction. A possible escape ploy I would proffer, though I may add this is not gleaned from personal experience, would be, immediately on rising from prolonged and torrid oral sex, to then collapse exhausted and sigh 'that was so good it seems I've come'. Whilst obviously still a disappointment this at least leaves the partner complimented.

NO GAME SHOW WILL EVER HOLD YOUR WORTH

I noticed on your windowsill
two broken flowers in a small glass
These were not set in pride of place but lay unassuming
like children huddled in the dark

Their stem too short now to fit the vase
convenience would have them dumped in a binliner
but something in you
could not let even this
seemingly dispensable
frail beauty die

I know such an action is no great gesture but only a tiny
moment in a far corner of the rush
but it is a victory
an everyday victory
and its colour should flutter within each heart

you, who are capable of such casual tenderness
what worlds your palms could describe
no game show will ever hold your worth
no computer ever measure your soul

whilst there is the merest glimmer of humanity
we are none of us lost

we are not lost

DAVID

David tries to do what's right
he just gets a little confused
he lives from moment to moment
he has the uneasy feeling that he's been used.
Proud to be an apprentice at 15
he didn't consider himself part of the production line
his college friends looked down on him, he knew that
since a child he'd entered the pool one foot at a time
and as his confidence grew, he stood for the union
he became more ambitious
he had a cause, a holy war
the injustice of big business.
Though young and angry
David tried to be a voice of sense
he would always seek a compromise
often at his own expense.
He said people want to do what's right
they're not sure which road to choose
he said you've got to do what you can
but I always sensed he felt he'd been used.

Some say he married fearing he was getting old
some say it was just a way of leaving home
when it ended they say it was mutual consent
but he cried like a baby all the same
he moved town, changed jobs
even tried changing his hair and his clothes
he forced himself to sit in pubs
and all night he'd drink alone.
Even at 30
he was entering the pool one foot at a time
he'll probably hold that fear
for the rest of his life
he said people want the best for you
we're all a little bruised
David says he's not bitter
but somehow I feel he's been used.

DONKEY AND THE OLD MAID

Guilt
Resentment
Unfulfilled ambition
Jealousy........

"The complete set,
Happy Family!"
declared the husband
laying his cards on the table.

"Happy Family?" puzzled the wife,
"I thought we were playing snap."

HAPPINESS

Happiness
is relative
a   distant   relative
the sort you see once a year
and can never stop long

BEAUTY AND THE INSECT HEART

The ocean is the wisest of councillors
Before its double moon
comforted by a mother's breath
I offer my heart as a small gift of stones
This is the closest I may get to perfection
   I saw a thousand shoes today but one pair of eyes
   Beyond our solar system we've discovered
   a million stars, but so far only one planet
Some distance along the shore line
I can see a young couple
They are easy and familiar
They have something
all my sullen romance cannot reach
There is no urgency now
only the hurting of a single truth
I would give everything, everything
to share such acceptance
Not just with anyone, not just in abstract
but vivid like the cleansing of pain
or the healing of fractured bone
Here I will soothe the night
Here I will help build a cathedral of words
Not for worship or inanimate passion
or another broken relic on a forgotten mound
but for someone, someone close, knelt alone
somewhere on a distant beach
offering her heart as a small gift of stones.
   Later, nursing the motorway North and home
   the sunrise whispers promises in a rear view mirror

STRIPPER GOES TOO FAR

Squeezing her voluptuous breasts she pouted
the front row sat erect
the climax they never doubted
they'd all come to expect
(but now a little extra)
pulling back her smile, she pulled her top lip
and slipped it over her head
the skull exposed, sheer and vile
veins ran worming purple and red
down over her shoulder the skin peeled onto the floor
now no-one tried to hold her, no-one squealed for more
then she tore out both of her mammary glands
the Joe on the front row had so craved
and taking one in each hand
she rubbed them into his face
next the flesh of her bottom she plucked from her torso
and placed on the Joe's knees
hadn't he got what he wanted but more so
you'd have thought he'd be pleased
finally she ripped out her womb by the fallopian tubes
and forced it down his throat
he seemed to lose his taste for sex abuse
so at least it ended on a happy note

WITHIN YOUR ARMS

If you were
            water
I would laze in your caress
and if you were fire
I would bathe in your passion

If you were air
I would breathe in your perfume
and if
        you were wool
I would wrap myself in your warmth

and
if you were
            darkness
I would lose myself in you
                        forever

A HEART WITH TWO LEFT FEET

In the game of love
he stands out on the wing
awaiting the ball
looking dangerous
until when finally the
ball is played to his feet
he panics under pressure
and kicks the ball into touch.

PLANT LIFE

The grass is not only greener
     on the other side of the hill
It will, so they say
     Be greener tomorrow than it is today

THERE IS LOVE AT FIRST SIGHT

There is wonder in attraction
the dancing of light on the retina
the alignment of atoms into form and substance
the perception of science as nature

Anatomy and biology raised to aesthetics and beauty
the tautness of flesh over muscle and frame
the way fabric clings to an outline
the contours of a rib cage
the tilt of a pelvis
the enticement of hollows and shadows
poise and the grace of texture

Colours and tones that blend and sculpt the imagination
the vulnerability of a neckline
the fragrance of moisture and the lure of intoxication
the glow of touch and the genius of the blood's energy
there is miracle in personality
there is wonder in attraction
there is love at first sight
I am already yours

VERTIGO

watching each step
weighing each balance
a loss of concentration
a missed chance
another l
            o
              v
                e

                   d
                  i
                    e
                      s

YOUR ROOM

You're painting your nails in your do-it-yourself bedsit coffin
cleaning your mug whilst still drinking your coffee
eating sleeping drinking and waiting
as the tears dry you're there repainting
cleaning up the dust that the hoover missed
never allowing anything to rust
nothing must, not in your room
nothing must die, nothing must decay
you're painting the mirrors
and painting the windows in your room
you're turning down the light, only shades of white
colour your room. Between brush strokes you're
hesitating. I know you're in there
I can hear you.
Painting

LIKE AN ARTIST TORTURED

You paint only self-portraits now
spilling your pain onto canvas
detailing your misery
colouring with blood
you paint yourself only naked now
staining sweat on your art
painting in tears, hanging your fears and regrets in public
making an exhibition of yourself.

THE 'REAL ME' EXCUSE

Adolf Hitler
took off his shoes and settled down to the tv
turning to Eva Braun he sighed,
"But they don't know the 'real me' ".

A FARCE IS STILL A FARCE EVEN WITH SUBTITLES

and she tells me she loves him
with her hand stroking my inner thigh
Her face is symmetrical and her sweat has a pleasant composition
We are exchanging pretty lies like cigarette cards
Stifling disinterest like two old soldiers between battles
The mutual gratification of animal lust seems a distinct possibility
We are both whores to romance
but it is all too predictable
There is no pilgrimage in her finger tips
only the musing of calculation
and I wonder if my face displays its weariness
Bone clumsy
an idle stubble scratches the sheen from her make up
There is no nourishment in these overtures
only the mechanics of anatomy, a series of shrugs
How can your blood race so fast
but your heart remain unmoved
I don't have to wait for the morning to hate myself
Pitiful and pathetic seem insults too well used to scald disgust
When I look into the mirror, if I concentrate on the centre
features of my face, I can see how I used to look in my teens
Is it guilt that's swollen my neck
or my face wrapping itself against the world ?
The desire to wipe the slate clean, to start a new jotter,
competes each day against the easier option to drown all vivid
images in maudlin and lay, before God's feet, face down in the
subway, stained with my own piss
As you can see I try my best to romanticise this predicament
but tacky affairs always remind me of cheap early seventies movies.

THE COUPLE NEXT DOOR — A SHARING EXPERIENCE

The couple in the flat next door are always considerate enough to save their arguments until it's time for bed.

This selfless gesture ensures that their intimate secrets, their sexual inadequacies, inferiority and persecution complexes, petty jealousies, childhood traumas, parental rejections, adolescent failings, perverse lust fantasics, unfulfilled animal needs, and their constant insecurity in the other's commitment to the relationship are all that much easier for us to enjoy.

The annoying thing is though that he insists on whimpering in a weak pathetic whine that's very difficult to make out. She on the other hand has perfect diction through a wide range of levels from full pitch screaming right up to violent hysterical frenzy, at which she is particularly entertaining. It seems a general rule for both that the logic content of the argument decreases in direct proportion to the volume and speed of delivery. Another annoying habit he has is that of speaking away from the adjoining wall and I get the feeling sometimes that he's a little embarrassed at what he's actually saying. She however grasps every opportunity to exploit this weakness and gain the upper hand by repeating his sentences word for word in the form of a very loud exclamation mark.

A problem they share jointly is the frequent compulsion to storm off into another room after a particularly good line. Other distractions include the unnecessarily long pauses often mistaken for a premature aborting of the conflict leaving both participants and spectators alike with a frustrating sense of anti - climax, and the sporadic fits of door banging that can so often surprise even the most careful of listeners causing any glass not firmly held to make that embarrassing smashing sound as it drops from your ear to the foot of the wall. Possibly the most pitifully pathetic and therefore the most interesting phase of the argument usually comes when he's ready to make up but she's not quite ready. For the next six or seven minutes he's apologetic and condescending, then after one too many rejections he suddenly blows his top stomping around and shouting such memorable classics as "I'm trying to be nice to you, you stupid prat!" I don't think he's actually ever hit her though she's been violent often unnervingly violent many times, but once I understand in desperation trying to disperse the anger he spat full in her face. You could tell from the immediate reaction that he knew even as it happened it was the worst thing he could do. Listening to two broken people crying in the night can suddenly make you feel very lonely. At this point I usually hug my girlfriend tight and thank God that tonight the argument was next door.

TOUCH

Smoke rising
in the rain
we live in the same world
but worlds apart
the tear
and the anger

the soul
and the heart

touch
but not with rules
touch
where you can

SHOULD TENDERNESS BECOME PLAGUE

Should tenderness become plague
glory in its infection
carry its contagion
and pray the germ is hereditary

AVOIDING COMMITMENT

avoiding commitment
you can't end every sentence
with 'or is it?'

or can you?

LOVE LIKE HELL

LOVE LIKE HELL

I have this theory that when you die your whole life is re-run like a
sensorama video and you have to sit through it all again, every second,
unedited, in a room with every friend and every relative that's been in the
least bit involved. Now depending on what sort of life you've led this
could be Heaven or it could be Hell. Think about it, everyone's going to
see those private moments, those very private moments: farting in the
bath; wiping bogies down the side of the armchair; every second of
indulgent masturbation.

All the pathetic lies you told exposed for all to see; all the naff chat-up
lines you used when you were a teenager, and still used later; all the
places you had sex when you still lived at home. The things you did to
get by; the way you justified it all to yourself and every really dumb-arsed
no-balls shit-for-brains mistake you ever made you'll have to watch yourself
make again.
But then
     maybe
          there'll be those moments of rare beauty; the moments of
tenderness; the times you cried because you messed up; the things you
meant to say; the questions in the mirror; the promises you made when
you first held your own child; the nights you comforted another's
despair; the time your lover's face glowed like beauty on fire; the times
you said "I love you" and believed your love would outlive the universe.
The time you first held in your stomach thinking no-one would notice,
and the regret in your eyes when you feared you were getting old. When
you couldn't sleep one night and lay awake sweating and praying you
didn't die before doing something, something, just something.

It's only a theory, and in my more optimistic moods I like to think that
maybe there'll be a pause and a rewind for the good moments, and a fast
forward for the rest.

FIG. 1 AND FIG.2 DISCUSS THE VALUE OF COLD SEX

Diagrams don't have headaches
never have a lousy day
are never self-conscious and
are always in perfect shape
diagrams don't mind sex cold
their sole purpose is to breed
closeness and affection
they don't really need
diagrams are never hurt
and
diagrams never bleed

ANIMATE PASSION

Romance pales in the predictable

Now is
always the time for something irrational

THE HOUSE IS NOT THE SAME SINCE YOU LEFT

The house is not the same since you left
the cooker is angry — it blames me
The TV tries desperately to stay busy
but occasionally I catch it staring out of the window
The washing up's feeling sorry for itself again
it just sits there saying "What's the point, what's the point?"
The curtains count the days
Nothing in the house will talk to me
I think your armchair's dead
The kettle tried to comfort me at first
but you know what it's attention span's like
I've not told the plants yet
they still think you're on holiday
The bathroom misses you
I hardly see it these days
It still can't believe you didn't take it with you
The bedroom won't even look at me
since you left it keeps it's eyes closed
all it wants to do is sleep, remembering better times
trying to lose itself in dreams
it seems like it's taken the easy way out
but at night I hear the pillows
weeping into the sheets.

PUPPY LOVE — A DOG'S LIFE?

Whatever happened to little Julie Bowers? She was classy.
I'd never seen anyone so clean, she must have washed every day. Proper
leather school satchel with the straps and buckles and everything, just
like in the Bunty comics. Not that I read Bunty comics, sometimes I cut out
the outfits on the back cover.
Luckily around this time I discovered masturbation, so I no longer had to
hang from playground equipment to achieve that pleasant tingling sensation
in my groin.
But Julie Bowers was above all that, she was classy.
She was the kind of girl who would never fool around behind the library
curtains. I was just a scruffy kid with snotty sleeves and hand-me-downs
from an older sister, our love could never be. She lived in the posh part
of the council estate where the houses had hedges too thick to dive
through. She was unattainable, a Goddess.
She had the complete set of felt-tip colours, the full range with the light
and dark brown. To her jigsaws were fun. She entered all the Blue Peter
competitions and she could read Look And Learn without faking it.
She was classy alright, something of a playground intellectual and I
respected her mind, though in my weaker moments I just wanted her to snog
me to a state of total exhaustion. That seductive overbite, the cute
turned-up nose, her neat ponytail, pleated skirt and those knee length
white socks, she knew how to drive a boy wild.
Yes she was classy, mind you round our way any girl who ate with her mouth
closed was considered classy.
What could I do? I tried to drown my sorrows in Taunton's cider but
developed chronic flatulence instead. Were these really to be the
happiest days of my life?

ONLY CHRISTMAS AND BIRTHDAYS BRING DEATH THIS CLOSE

Overnight
you have grown old
and though spite is no spur to succeed
in the absence of caress it can suffice

Only yesterday with hair dye and vitamins
you boasted you had cheated time
but now
it is the last dance of the party and
the prospect of a taxi home alone
rises like a flush within your cheeks

Years you wasted slip through the
doorway giggling together adolescent
Clear skin and eyes so bright
and always with partners that look such fools, but young
It is not them you hate but their youth
There is no individuality in this attraction merely the
aesthetics of innocence

and you, clinging to that one chance
force yourself into the night air before
the indignity of being the last to leave

I have seen you in the morning
lost in some mundane task
unaware of my presence
There is a subtlety of emotion that wisps around your eyes
You hesitate behind each door
    What worries you most is the loss of appetite
Where once you were so sure,
    diplomatic farewells have beaten back your pride
Where once you were curious,
    the nakedness of longing has sought to scar your faith
breathe still
breathe still
no whim of nature will chill your soul tonight

there are traditions that carry the truth of seasons
there are books that will outlast technology
we are old friends you and I
rest your fears against these words
it'll be alright
it will be alright.

LET'S PRETEND

Let's pretend we're both drunk and you're not married
and I'm not courting that girl in the kitchen and nobody
can see us and we don't know what we're doing and you put
your hand down my trousers whilst I lick your nipples and
if anyone comes in and finds us we were only pretending.

And because it's dark we can pretend to fumble about and
grope at each others crotch and buttocks and you can drape
your knickers over my head whilst I bend you over the chair
and if people should say anything we can pretend it was only
innocent party games and when we sink to the ash stained
carpet exhausted and unkempt we can pretend it was great and
even that we share something special and then you can go back
to your husband and I to my girlfriend and pretend.

LOVE TURNED GREEN

She inflicted her love like a wound
and only with her hand laid on the wound
and only when it wept did she have faith in her love
it was a love that cowered in doorways
a love that talked in accusations
where the words "I love you" became a threat
and where love hung like terror over every chance remark.

THIS LAND OF EQUAL OPPORTUNITY

A patch of dirt on his mother's skirt he clings on to save his life
A passenger in her frustration dragged past the age of five
Not for him the fairy land
He's taught right and wrong by the back of the hand
His life is planned inbred at birth
The urban waste of a council estate his first taste of Mother Earth
Told to sit as soon as he could crawl
The fiction in the picture books don't fit his life at all
And his mind begins to wonder what lies behind the high school wall
His mother can't wait to placate him
She lays more sugar on his dummy
"Work harder" says his father, "you too could soon earn money."
If it wasn't so sad it might just be funny
He sees his parents lie and cheat
Then discovers the other face they displace on the street
He's being taught the basic language of corruption and deceit
Used as a hostage in their petty rows
Abuse of a child is not reviled in the marriage vows
So thrown against the fridge in silence he looks
At violence and pain unknown in his kiddies story books
Now they've traded the dummy for the TV
The teacher asks him what he wants to be
He never mentions a job on the factory floor
But then neither did his father some thirty years before
With dreams scraped from the TV screen
And a start in life best forgot
In this land of equal opportunity
What chance has he really got?

THERE'S ALWAYS ROOM IN THE HEARSE ON THE WAY BACK

Joseph plays the percentages.
He can be eyeing up four women in different parts of
the same room.
He takes his data day diary literally.
A wall chart of his sperm level would read like a cardiac arrest.
To him Love is a dog with six legs.
Relationships, just things that crash in the night.
Loyalty, a free fall from infatuation to indifference.
From the erotic to the erratic.

There is a need to prove that he can still compete.

To Joseph
Nature gives no time to niceties.
Forever, comes with in-built obsolescence.
There always appears a point in coupling when he feels like
he's stuck next to someone on a long coach journey having ran
out of conversation.

In despair, it is of course the things we don't say that shout
the loudest.
Joseph mutilates his every hour.
I don't believe he chooses to be ugly
it is merely an ailment
a sickness of the spirit.

Joseph's crime is that of cowardice.
He has spent his whole life running with the eye of the storm
and destiny seems such a big word for such a small return.

Cranking up suspense in adolescence
   the pivot and swerve
   the running of the escalator
   carnal desire his internationalle
Joseph shys away from the need of a meaning

For the ultimate taboo is to be lonely.
   even for a second
   and so to fail
   to be an object of pity
   to be a loser
and cliches become cliches for a reason
no-one, but no-one, loves a loser.

It is to strands of this
he ties his final submission.
   Hoping as mortality yawns.
   Hoping as the sediment thaws.
   Hoping as the essence pulls immediate to his breath
that his lies
are lies
after all.

LOVE BY LIST

You're new to my list of acquaintances
let us list the things we have in common
I like your lists — here are a list of good points I've spotted
here is a list of things for us to say, and a list of other lists that
will come in handy.

I love you, see under list no.14
for response.
You are not responding correctly
have you read your lists? Here is a
list of things you are doing wrong.
Here is another list, you will see some
items have been duplicated.

I'm afraid I've lost the list with
your good points, but it's OK
I'm too busy keeping all these
lists together.

I'm going to have to
take you off my list of active
relationships, still don't worry
I have a list for you
we can put you here under failures.

THE TROUBLE WITH THERESA

Theresa wants desperately to be loved
She flings her arms around the world
as if to say "I love you, why won't you love me?"
Theresa tries too hard to be accepted
Within minutes of meeting her
she'll have told you her entire life story
she'll have squeezed your arm
she'll have bought you a drink.
Theresa sees all her own faults but no-one else's
she needs constant reassurance
she finds relationships never last but
she's never the one to break up; no matter what
she clings on and clings on tight,
as if to say "I love you, why won't you love me?"
The trouble with Theresa is she desperately wants to be loved
that's the trouble with Theresa
that's the trouble.

NEED

If need was currency
          who could buy you from me?

THE POEM I HOPE I SHALL NEVER WRITE CALLED ENGLAND

The poem I hope I shall never write called England, has 60
million pairs of sensible shoes, written in co-ordinated
pastels, it smiles a Dale Carnegie smile between the lines of
500 miles of dark blue pinstripes.

With a meal ticket for the gravy train you pay 6 Hail Mary's
and say you are just trying to get through, but is it ever
enough just to get through?

Dehumanised by the doberman mentality, behind the turrets of
the neighbourhood watch, I see the dust on the lustre of the
Emerald Isle and small swastikas on the latest liberty prints.
To the court of St James - never mind the product feel the
lifestyle. The writing on the wall bids you welcome to Hotel
Earth where as precious as poetry you hold up your life to the
light and find it ornate like a hollow vase or a pale thin
complexion, until shards of conscience kick sand in your suntan
lotion and you suffer with all the political depth of a
designer sweatshirt. It's the gospel according to St Michael
carrier bags. I breath in - Whig history and the uncivil list,
Cathedral cities wringing their hands, invisible earnings and
the bank of opinion tells me throw another miner on the
barbecue.

Meanwhile . . . . . .
                    back at reality . . . . . .
                                        the divisions blister

I see old men asking for ten pence outside multi-million pound
shopping centres, carboard box bedouins bowing to the power of
the rota blades, bamboo Babel and the American wet dream.
Diluting to taste, Gazza attempts the futility of the Sun
crossword, I drank the world T shirt, unzips a grin, draws a
Hitler moustache on a Harrier jump jet, Benny Hill burgers for
breakfast, going down for the third time, sucking plankton, I
breath in - Bingo culture, Smallville UK, Mr wet underpants 1989,
Death Valley Amusements and 10 pints of frogspawn. To the
court of St James - there's a view from any train pulling through
the backstreets of any Northern town calling you liar.
By the tomb of the unknown shopper another lorry dumps 2 tons
of ear wax on the wrong lawn and a fat tongue comes on the
radio, it says 'sorry but . . sorry but . . sorry but . . (click).

At the end of your clean clothes chain in Anorak, tank top,
shorts and odd socks, on the way to the launderette you say
you're just trying to get through, but is it ever enough just
to get through? To the court of St James - there's blood on
your pages. I can almost see the stains on the white white
cliffs as we near the coast of the poem I hope I shall never
write called England.

A GIFT

At 7 o'clock this morning
I bring you a mountain
I tap gently on your window
and you wake half covered in sleep.

"What's that?" you ask
"It's a mountain" I grin,
"I've carried it all night
I couldn't sleep so I brought it
here to show you."
"What do I want with a mountain in my garden at 7 o'clock in the
morning?" you ask, not used to being woken at 7 o'clock with a
mountain in your garden.

I try to joke, now feeling a little embarrassed,
"It's for you, a gift."
You say you don't want a mountain.
You are too tired to understand,
and I struggle to explain it's not the mountain I've brought you
it's the fact that I could bring it to you.
I strain to pick it up again and wonder what I'm going to do with it now.
I feel such a fool walking home with a mountain.

HOW THE YOUNG AND FASHIONABLE ARE FEELING THIS SEASON

They're wearing their
consciences well hid
this season. Hearts on
the sleeve are definitely
out. Compassion's out.
Basically the effect is not
to distract attention
from the expensive clothes.

SEX BEFORE PARENTS

A parent expects
their son to have sex
but not so their daughter
true values they've taught her.

But with their double standard logic
they never seem to have thought of
the fact their son sleeps around
with other parent's daughters.

LIKE BOB HOPE AND BING CROSBY IN "ROAD TO PUBERTY"

When I was 15 I used to have a friend,
he was my best friend.............and I hated him.
He had perfect teeth
and he always won on the slot machines
just after I'd been on and lost;
he was my best friend..........and I hated him.
He was a little older than me
so I used to tell his girlfriends
his teeth were false.
When they kissed him they'd try and lick the inside of
his gums and he'd think they were being sexy.
I told them he wore a toupee as well
and they'd run their fingers through his hair
and he'd smile away — the daft bastard.
He was better than me at everything
but he was my best friend.............and I hated him.
And I hated myself for hating him
which made me hate him even more.
I'd call him sanctimonious —
and he'd forgive me.
It's said you like people for their good points
but you love them for their faults
and he never had any faults —
apart that is from his choice of best friend,
and for that I suppose I loved him.

SUZANNE

She's never come to terms with her shape
or been comfortable with any of her hairstyles

the clothes she hangs herself in never hold the person
she feels she wants to see in the mirror

no matter how she sits she feels awkward
she doesn't like the summer, it casts shadows on her face

she says her face is too angular that's the problem
tight fitting clothes make her feel disproportionate

she never looks how she feels
maybe she's getting old, she thinks.

WHEN HOMES BECOME HOUSES

You can't be too careful these days
now love is riddled with herpes
and crippled with A.I.D.S.
So I've taken to wearing a durex over my head, just in case.

I've put a durex over the cat
a durex over the car
and although it reduces sensitivity
it makes perfect sense to me
last night I put a durex over my heart

Love is,
        now a durex bed with durex pillows
we live in a durex house with nailed down windows
we speak only through sanitized phones, durex extra safe
and we want to be buried in a six foot durex, in separate graves.

INTERNAL MEMO

Forget big business

the only holding company
I want
is you

THE MUTUALLY ASSURED DESTRUCTION OF MR. AND MRS. JONES

Like most arguments neither can remember who fired the first shot.
Both still had snipers positioned from their previous confrontations.
Both had started to build entrenchments. This time though it had
escalated into open conflict on a scale never seen before.
Mr. Jones was flexing his muscles.
Mr. Jones was about to demonstrate who wore the trousers.
Mrs. Jones was beating the shit out of him.
In the aftermath there followed a period of chilled silence.
This Mr. and Mrs. Jones referred to as the cold war.
They built a wall between them. At first friends dropped in supplies.
Each began developing new weapons to inflict pain upon the other.
Each labelled their weapons "deterrents."
Each was determined if need be to "deterrent" the other into oblivion.
Then gradually as paranoia became a firm enough basis to build upon
peace talks began.
But if one day either of their tongues should slip....

THE REFLECTION IN THE BACK OF GOD'S SPOON

Nude modelling for the afterlife
she secures the burger concession in Paradise

It's difficult to be concerned at the world's wrongs
with an industrial base of cream scones

There are dead moths at your alter
Theme parks replacing the landscapes of human nature

There's an empty funhouse with a formica carousel
A gardener nurturing humanity on the high road to Hell

Originality for the mass market reaped with a vengeance
individually wrapped tears and brutal indifference

As reproach stalks this poetry in thin disguise
for dogs bound by pavement there is little pride

All the seas of Mercy yet to understand
I feel the sadness of computers in an enchanted land

How can the Mortician fill dead bodies with formaldehyde
then go home and make love to his wife?

The wasting of limbs and the squandering of belief
Perpetual emotion and the dignity of trees
It's fear of death
beating the wings of my heart
I reach for your hand in the dark
I reach for your hand in the dark

THE FIRST FRACTURE OF INNOCENCE IS THE HATCHING OF ALL REGRET

Ours is a strange love affair
The only Magpie left to mourn
   is phantom upon my back

His song laments his long lost mate
He tells me he will cling to me even in dreams
He will circle my burial
   even as the prayers fall away
He will brood forever over my scratch of earth

For ours is a strange love affair
   yet without his faith in instinct
who else could understand how sweet were once
   the purest notes of joy

Imperfection itself should grieve
   to have suffocated such a tiny breath
no parchment can ever dress this wound
or weeping ever wash even the smallest regret from the land
Death is a burden clasped on every back

And ours is a strange love affair
Punishment to shame remorse
Sorrow already perched on an empty grave

TRAVELLING SECOND CLASS THROUGH HOPE

With softer spine you rise and shine
And strap yourself safe in time
More beads for the natives, more gongs for the troops,
You buy off the kids with spaghetti hoops
Melt into the monotone, the drip-feed TV
Death Wish 4, Funland UK, until you say
Is   this   all   there   is   ?

You say you need a cause, you need to fight
You're looking for something, anything
If only you had something noble denied
You say sometimes you'd fight everything
So down at the beast market
You seek solace in your crisps
Hey what's a nice Jaeger jumper like that
Doing in a place like this?
You see Madonna singing "Material Girl"
To earthquake victims in The Third World
You see a white car drive through Soweto
Swords designed as shields
The new credit card diplomacy
And the worship of God on wheels, and you say
Is   this   all   there   is   ?

And when the party's over, and limp lettuce and lager trodden into the
carpet are no longer part of the fun. And you realise that the Earth
doesn't revolve around three pubs in the centre of town. And you realise
your God's not bigger than my God after all. Travelling second class
through Hope, you pray, there must be more than this.

THE LADIES' MAN

He poured the word darling like acid
It ate
Through
Nameless
Women
Faceless
As the acid
Scoured
The flesh
From the bone
Darling — it smarted, keen to the touch
Darling — it stung, as it seeped into the conversation
He poured the darling like acid
Saying "Don't worry your pretty little head now
        Don't worry your pretty little head."

PRAGMATIC ROMANTICISM

1. ... for want of a better word we call it love.

With your leg bent over mine I can feel the moistness of your desire.
With your breast cupped against my lifeline I can feel the
flourish of your heart.
There is a dance within your pulse.

2.   Some days I lay in bed all morning waiting for the phone to ring.

I could get up but I need outside intervention. Some stimulus, catalyst, impetus,
the door bell to buzz, the landlord to knock, the window cleaner to bruise his lad-
ders against the paintwork, a poster to fall from the wall, the bedroom to burst into
flames, anything.
I am already dead, my carcass exhumed to imitate devotion
Some days I close my eyes and lay my heart off the hook.

3.   Though the world now lays empty
        as the dialogue in a cheap porn movie

        Once. Maybe.
        On another continent
        where the sky seemed wider
        allowing arms to stretch out and loosen the joints.
There
without fear of declaring our love
we held hands across a culture
like two mirrors turned inwards
reflecting a private eternity.
If there is no such thing as true love then all logic is built
on the smallest unit of time.

THE ACCIDENTAL DEATH OF A CAT

Outside the polling office
I saw a cat that had never voted
run over by a man made machine
that failed to notice

Like a circus crowd
a random cross-section of the electorate
as if being entertained by a performing poodle
spectated, as spasms of pain
jerked the body into acrobatics.

Someone went to phone . . but to phone who?
Someone went to find the owner.
Someone went for a half brick.

the cat lay still at last, one eye dangling loose
like a battered old teddy bear.
The half brick was discarded.
The cat placed reverently into a Safeways carrier bag.

The afternoon sun dried the small smudges of blood
into the tarmac.
The colours meshed so that soon you
could hardly notice the difference
when you passed.
Later that night all parties claimed victory.

THE SONG

While
       some people
       find joy
       humming along
    to the enchanting music of the song

Others
       listen closely
       to the words
       trying to comprehend
    the true meaning of the song

but sadly
       not all the words are audible

THE LAST POEM I EVER WROTE

The last poem I ever wrote I had such high hopes for.
The last poem I ever wrote was to have been so powerful it would make
war obsolete and nuclear fusion as vital as trainspotting. It was to
have been so cleverly constructed it would hold the key to the
very universe itself, make Arthur C. Clarke redundant and James Burke
intelligible; so full of life it would be strapped onto wounds, and made
into tablets and ointment. The Olympic committee would disqualify
competitors found to have read it. Laid over the face of a child's corpse
it would bring the dead back to life.
The last poem I ever wrote was published in a low budget poetry
magazine boasting a print run of 220, 150 of which still remain under
the editor's bed. The title escapes me but it was some pathetic pun
such as "Write Now."
The last poem I ever wrote was performed to an alternative cabaret
audience at Cleethorpes off-season in between an alternative juggler and
a 22-piece Catalonian dance band. Coinciding with the call for last
orders it was heckled constantly by a drunk born and bred in London who
sang in a scotch accent and claimed to own the city of Glasgow
personally.
The last poem I ever wrote was entered in a poetry competition by a
lifelong enemy. The judges having been certified dead were suitably
appointed as their names were unknown even to each other let alone to
anyone else. My poem came 63rd out of 7 million entries and won a
year's subscription to the Crumpsall Poetry Appreciation Society
Crochet Circle and Glee Club Gazette.
The last poem I ever wrote was cremated along with my body, unread.
The last poem I ever wrote was carried in the hearts of those I loved.

St VALENTINE'S RESTS NOT ON THE CALENDER BUT IN THE HEART

New friends tell me I've become disfigured in repartee
that all softness or aggression is passe
that detachment is sophistication
To think it should come to this
To think it should come to this

(Her eyes were emerald and there was a simple joy in watching
her brush her hair)
As if bewitched by childhood
I have seen you dazzle
I have lightened my frown to the bond of sweethearts
I have chanced the whirlwind of derision
And as enchantment ends
on yet another carriage I cower from
Chinese whispers that taunt floodlights on my illusions

. . . sometimes I wonder if I've ever been in love
it's like trying to explain why a joke is funny

No matter how I feign indifference, I still fear flying
As each plane leaves the ground my prayers are of you
If the soul survives I want above all to hold your presence
This may not weigh heavy in the glib torrent of conversation
but at times such as these those moribund do not lie, not to themselves

I realise to you I am already fable
It seems I lost you even before we met
. . . don't look at me now I've grown old and ugly whilst you remain
breathless as a new constellation.

SORRY

"Sorry" is a small word only five letters
that is four different letters and one swap
having two letter 'r's.

"I love you" is three small words
eight letters, that is seven and one swap
the letter 'o'.

"I forgive you" is two small words and a fairly
small word, eleven letters, ten and one swap.

I'll exchange you one of my most valuable
"sorry's" and an almost priceless "I love you"
that's thirteen letters in all, if you say
"I forgive you."

Of course, if you want to throw in an "I love you too,"
we can really start talking business.

DOES INFLATION AFFECT THE EMOTIONS ?

TIME PASSED UNNOTICED UNTIL SHE TOOK THE CLOCK

Slumped on your chair like dead weight at an orgy
coughing like an 'S' reg Fiat
though you've lit up a thousand churches in prayer
you know
         she's not coming back

Overfat on time, you say 'age doesn't matter' then you lie about your own
if you live to be 100 you'd still be afraid of dying too young
Switching off the bedside lamp shadows crowd the void
but the patterns on the wallpaper don't scare you anymore
it's the blank spaces now that threaten
Nothing, not even love, survives within a vacuum

Fast approaching your love-by date
you count the days left unkissed
Age
    has become just another stick to beat yourself with
Where once your passion was an elevator between Heaven and Hell
Where once you believed love dripped from between her legs
There in the absence of children
sex grew tired on easy living, becoming a parasite on the back of routine
        and all the words you chose so carefully
blew like so much litter
Conversations became quieter
and as scarce as in a spaghetti western
Laughter became a missing person
until you couldn't remember kissing her face when you last made love
and her lips became just hooks to hang your heart upon
and though you look for that face from the window of every train
the photo in your pocket is now starting to fade
and though you curse the new diary with each year that arrives
you never noticed the clock on the wall until it kissed you goodbye
you never noticed the clock on the wall until it kissed you goodbye

THE COLLECTIVE GUILT OF THE GOLDEN HANDSHAKE

If only I could I would rip out my bloodline
by wrenching every vein from my body
that I might cleanse myself
of this inbred apathy
I saw the best minds of my generation destroyed by
Madness, Ultravox and Spandau Ballet

I had the heart of a great poet
but never the Oxbridge intellect
I felt the shadows of clouds on mountains
and the firmness of flesh during sex
but Byron, Keats and Shelley
never made me laugh like Jack Benny

Red rag to a bull
red flag to a radical
from comedian to chameleon
lounge lizard by nightfall
hush now the Pied Piper's playing our tune
do not go gently into that Jean Paul Gaultier suit

Fidelity is of little importance
left wing romance - a fickle dance
how many ears have you got to cut off
before somebody listens
St George just caused one dragon to fall
Jesus himself only made one curtain call

Suddenly - the Japanese bomb Cheetham Hill with videos
Prince Phillip bows to Hirohito
the nodding dogs of capitalism
close ranks on the commuter line
the square on the hi-fi
is equal to the sum of the squares on the other two sides

It's 1939, and they're already killing the first born
all's laissez faire in love and war, and football
it's the first three rounds to Goliath
it's a cause without a rebel
only this morning David knelt beside the stream
and took out 5 pebbles

I love you Daddy Warbucks - roll the credits

ALL KIDS ARE BORN WITH LONG THIN MOUSTACHES

Like most kids I suppose I was a natural surrealist.

I used to think nothing of playing football for hours in my cowboy outfit.
I had no concept of relative scale and no distinct understanding of the
comparative relationship between any two objects.
My Action Man would regularly hitch lifts straddled across a 2 inch
Matchbox fire engine.
Toilet rolls, shoeboxes, Elastoplast reels, coat hangers and Fairy Liquid
bottles were all stock multi-faceted components to fit into any imaginary
playworld.
But never, and I always felt this to be one of the major drawbacks to my
creativity, the double-sided sticky tape Blue Peter and Magpie presenters
somehow always assumed you'd have lying around. For years I pictured all
middle class kids having drawers full of the stuff.
Large cardboard boxes could change in seconds from racing cars to jet
planes or speed boats just by a slight alteration in the accompanying
engine noise.
Any sheet or table cloth became a tent which I'd just sit in for days and
days and days.
One of my very favourite games was when the British 8th Army desert patrol
Airfix soldiers would fight off the alien spaceship which was always made
out of Lego and manned by Fuzzy-Felt farm animals.

TRUE COLOURS

The roots of my underlying personal philosophy and my political perception could well go back to around the age of 8.
For football at Hogarth primary school we'd tend to divide roughly into red shirts versus blue shirts.
But my Aunt Margaret had given me an old Blackburn Rovers shirt she'd bought cheap at a jumble (purple and black chequered).
Strangely enough I was the only kid with a Blackburn Rovers shirt, but then we did live in Nottingham which I always felt was a good test of a true Rovers supporter. Most of the other kids would naturally display allegiance to their favourite heroes Man. United, Forest or Liverpool, Man City or Chelsea pretending to be George Best or Rodney Marsh or whoever.
I was always Ralph Ironmonger, possibly Blackburn's finest ever left back.
What the other kids failed to recognise was that although they were committed to a definite side I still had the freedom of choice. I could play for the reds or the blues. I could even swap sides half way through... without telling anyone. I sometimes wonder if my Aunt Margaret was secretly an anarchist.

THE GLAISDALE SCHOOLYARD ALLIANCE OF 1974

At school
Valerie, Debby and Netta
were the best of friends

but
you'd never see all three of them together
only ever two at a time
always having fell out with the third
Val and Debby together
then Val and Netta
then Debby and Netta

At school
Valerie, Debby and Netta
were the best of friends
they all hated Sandra Vickers

DAD'S SHOES

Shining Dad's shoes was my first real responsibility
a task I took very seriously, eager to impress
like an apprentice adult.

Very few memories of Dad come to me now from my early childhood.
I'm sure he was there
but always it seems standing at the back slightly out of focus.
I remember his old jacket weighed down with betting slips
as if all the chances he had ever missed were gradually dragging him back
bent gravebound.
I remember being proud that as a youth he'd had trials for Derby County.
I remember too the gravity of being caught giggling behind the settee during
the pools check.
I remember once being scolded for having caught nits
and I remember more than once sitting on the stairs in the dark having been
sent to bed before 'The Man From U.N.C.L.E.'
Now I don't actually remember getting the blame for when my elder sister
put the Horlicks jar down her knickers causing it to smash on the pavement,
but I'm told I did.

I do remember though one day after school whilst waiting for a lift home
I'd just taken a bit of a chance and had darted into the sweetshop for an
orange Jubilee when at that precise moment Dad passed by in his car
completely unaware of my presence
I ran and ran
all the way into the living room
up to his chair beside the fire
heart pumping
fighting for breath
anxious to explain that we had only just missed each other
It's now 23 years later and I'm still running

VERBAL WALLPAPER

Some talk self-interest

Some talk confusion

Some talk questions

Some talk statements

Some talk anger

Some talk wonder

Some talk trivia

Hardly ever do we translate

AN EARLY CAREER MOVE

The first major decision of my life occurred
age 12 at my very first disco; The William Sharp Bilateral end of term
Christmas party, held at 6.30pm in the school gym.
No longer just kids stuff - a proper DJ with twin turntables, two flashing
lights and the very latest in high-tec ... fluorescent tubing — this was
the real thing.

It wasn't until I finally braved the dance floor that I realised the tweed
jacket was a mistake. What was worse I'd recently had one of my front teeth
capped and I was still so proud of my new smile I never once suspected that
under the fluorescent lighting I suddenly bore an uncanny resemblance to a
rabid escapee from Watership Down. Then, what with a chronic case of
dandruff as yet unchecked by family Vosene and here agitated with one too
many epileptic renditions of my much acclaimed and often requested Spotty
Dog impression to the accompaniment of such classics as 'Chirpy Chirpy
Cheep Cheep', I realise now I must have looked like a one-man science
fiction horror laser show. An acned pubescent pocketsize Jean Michel
Jarre.

Needless to say I wasn't a big hit with the girls that night. Not even my
eventual mastery of the essential Hank Marvin three step circular dance
routine could salvage my waning sex appeal.

It was recoiling from a chance glimpse of my reflection in a nearby
mirrored surface that a career in comedy first presented itself as a likely
alternative to that of romantic lead. A wise decision in one so young but
then as I was to learn over and over again acute embarrassment has a
marvellous effect of concentrating the mind.

MIXED METAPHORS

Upon recognition
an outburst of enthusiasm
and then
we'd probably struggle to find something in common
Old friends lost in the shuffle
seeking points of reference, as awkward as mixed metaphors
with words like anticlimax and disappointment lurking in the wings
but even so
I'd still like us to meet up again someday, ideally in passing
when rushing for a train
with just enough time to test the water
sketch in the bare bones of a future conversation and most importantly, in
case we never meet again, to say
those simple but difficult things we should, but never do, say
consoling ourselves with phrases like 'taken as read' or 'can't be put into
words'
Those most important of things never said but just drowned in the moment
and lost in the shuffle

THE ACME GOD COMPANY

Higher purchase with a higher purpose
Paradise privatized like a three ring circus
Heaven on high at down to Earth prices
Sell yourself right out of a crisis
Sell yourself something you already own
for the Father and the Son are just a family firm
and lo
        the word of the Lord on the big board is quoted
as the Holy Spirit is finally floated
it's a preference share for Armageddon
see how the Dow Jones closes at Psalm one hundred and eleven
and behold
        the soul is sold from the National Health
so the poor that can't pay can go straight to Hell

and the Lord looked down on his Cherubim
lain broken on the ground with ruptured wings
and he wept

LOOKING FOR A SWEETER COCKTAIL

I see kids asleep on piss stained sheets
someone's dad sick-drunk on a 60 bus
towels that smell of damp
buttons hanging and zips bust
I see slack pillowslips at Christmas with nothing to fill them but a
stomach full of tears
These are the ghosts of the Christmas present for nearly 2000 years
Looking for a sweeter cocktail fantasy returns to favour
reality tasted neat has a very bitter flavour
My Tupperware runneth over, your Hush Puppies are barking mad
there's a million ways we deceive ourselves
even God wears a silly hat
It's shopping as a multiple orgasm
It's the I'm alright jackboot
Whenever the word society hits the conversation
then you know it's time to bail out
It's a land of beggars and hypocrites
South African goods in the Asian shop
If the capitalism fits - wear it
It's survival - but survival of what?
Looking for a sweeter cocktail fantasy returns to favour
reality tasted neat has a very bitter flavour
Looking for a sweeter cocktail the hour's too late to sleep
with a prayer for all that will not fade
we touch softly on the cheek
with a prayer for all that will not fade
we kiss softly on the cheek
and for a moment in a world of moments
the cocktail for once tastes sweet.

THE LURE OF THE SALMON SANDWICH

To Seymour Street return I ought t'
swimming upstream against the water
though the 39 bus
is a lot less fuss
and makes the journey shorter

SHOPPING IN PARADISE

You measure your success
by counting the things you'll never have
The yardstick you used
is sold in all the main stores in town
They sell hundreds each week
on the never never

HELL IS A PLACE WHERE ALL THE PHOTOS YOU THOUGHT YOU'D SAFELY DESTROYED ARE ENLARGED

Yesterday
all the litter that I'd threw away throughout my life
came round to visit me.
It demanded to be let in
said we needed to talk.
Feeling guilty at the ease with which I'd so conveniently discarded it
I let it in.
There hardly seemed room for it all.
The used tea bags alone filled the kitchen and there were margarine tubs
and toe-nail clippings I hadn't seen for ten years or more.
Strange now to think how they used to be very much part of my life at one
time.
I confess I found it difficult to relate.
I've changed a lot. I'm sure some of the litter has changed. It's bound to
have. The half used tin of tomatoes from April 1964 certainly had.
A chipped mug with no handle took the initiative, it asked why I never
rang, 'I kept meaning to', I lied 'but I've lost the number'.
The number itself cowered on a screwed up piece of paper and said nothing.
Sharing the same piece of paper the words 'I'm sure we can still be good
friends' blushed like felt tip.
Several old shoes, a left handed glove, a recent batch of razor blades and
numerous bread wrappers each with one crust left in began to edge round
the topic of coming back. The remains of an Airwick solid opened up trying
to clear the air. The atmosphere was getting a little uncomfortable. A few
old fly papers conceded that they had never really held out much hope and
had only come along with the rest.

There was an awkward silence when I introduced the new bin bags.
Eventually I managed to persuade all but one or two Piccalilli jars that
coming back maybe wasn't such a good idea
and after a few hours we parted amicably enough.
I don't think there'll be any further visits, for a while at least, even so
I don't know that I like the way the swing bin now looks at me, knowingly.

STATE OF THE HEART

Who is it quickens your heart
                    when the phone rings ?
Who's company makes you giggle
                    without the need for drinks ?

Who do you dream of when the firelight is yours ?
Who's name do you whisper behind
                    your bedroom door ?
Who do you want to share your silences ?

A MORE INTIMATE FAME

She licked the applause from the fingers of each hand
 like honey drips from toast
but could never hold on tight enough
 to that for which she hungered most
Only let into the heart like a holiday home
 though always a paying guest
Scratching for dignity from blind hope
 but knowing dignity is still second best
Love has always been one of those rooms at parties
 that she'd never dare venture inside
where close friends sat cross-legged on floorboards
 and she had no invite
Always outstretched arms at railway stations
 into which she'd never run
or couples on buses in matching jumpers unashamed to dress as one
This time though she thought she'd sneaked unnoticed into the
 gates of heaven - Accepted for her sins
but she clung too tight never understanding
 how fragile a thing are wings
and when the regret welled up inside
 there was no cradle for her soul and her broken pride
 How can it hurt so much if the love has died ?
and soon all the narrow eyes and shallow lives
 became a noose around her neck
until accelerating into fog the drink cocooned her head
 how can you love so much
 how can you love so much
 how can you love so much and have nothing left ?

A REPORT FROM THE FRONT

Each step I take closer   I'm more unsure
am I making mistakes   that I made before ?
your heart is a weapon   your love is a war
you smokescreen your emotions
                                         are my advances getting through ?
like flying blind   over World War Two
I'm walking a minefield to you

Booby traps trip   your inner defences
your no-mans land   is enforced with trenches
the flag you fly   says no surrender
though hostilities have ended   with peace talks in view
the most dangerous steps   are the very last few
I'm walking a minefield to you

I'm
      walking
a
                 minefield
    to
you

FLUNKING THE PRACTICAL

It's easy to see now I must have upset the upset the spontaneity of the occasion a little, leaping from bed after 3 and a half minutes extensive foreplay and rushing to the toilet there to wrestle with a Durex for the better part of an hour, but being inexperienced and easily embarrassed and knowing no better at the time it all seemed perfectly justified.

Once alone in the toilet I fumbled frantically in an effort to don my little passion accessory, my sexual fervour now waning fast due in no small measure to the cold toilet seat, the fact that it was her parents toilet, the less than romantic atmosphere of the white woodchip walls and do-it-yourself plumbing, the ever lengthening gap in our mutual arousement and having tried unsuccessfully to roll the strange accoutrement on the wrong way twice, further blunting my ardour and leaving me with a task not dis-similar to stacking custard or trying to thread jelly into a pair of Doc Martens.

When eventually I slipped surreptitiously back under the blankets my sexual initiation re-commenced cautiously. Although I'd taken a keen interest in the theory aspect at school there were still one or two points they were never too specific about in sex education classes.

Not mentioning that the sperm doesn't just disappear but can run back down a girl's leg when she stands up was one. The most important omission as far as I was concerned however was not explaining exactly how long the coitus activity should generally take. For 4 hours we hammered away trying to make sure that the job was done right. I didn't want her to think that I wasn't adequately potent and she didn't want to let on that she'd had enough 3 and a half hours since. All the next day we walked around exhausted and bruised, tender and inflamed, recovering from what felt effectively like a 4-hour Chinese burn on the genitals.
I marvelled at friends who boasted that they did it every night thinking they must have really suffered.

CONVERSATION ITSELF NEED NOT CONSUMATE CONCERN
A MOTHER AND CHILD DO NOT FRAME THEIR LOVE IN WORDS

I am sitting with you again

As usual you are courting solitude
You are browsing possible lifestyles
        and though I am troubled by the vivid contrast
I will not discolour this silence
The fiction of your presence is communication enough

Of course, I am, I know, creating my own fantasy
My imagination needing only the allure of your femininity as
transport
        Lost within your glossy magazine
        colour co-ordinated rooms do not allow
        for the frailty of the hesitant
        and the self conscious
        These images of intellect can never offer the softness
        of promise
        that soothes the hurt and carries
        the simplicity of a child's drawing
        within even the boldest of hearts
I will try to fake nonchalance when your eyes eventually
look up from the page

In the time it takes
for a breath to change from inward to outward
we are re-writing a new future
I am sitting with you again
You are somewhere where the stars offer different possibilities
but there is no distance between us.

SEXUAL POLITICS AND THE RELUCTANT ANARCHIST

You cannot give yourself
to this moment
There is an element of courage and charity
                    in each kiss you allow

Now all movements are within
and the alignments are not so clear
The responsibility of control
and the struggle for compromise between
possibility and fulfilment
   blur the majority verdict of collective morality
        and the expectations of others often too
                    removed to court justice

I have come to the belief that there is no right but
                    the submission to desire
Though this, I've learnt, is an acquired notion
        embroidered on the scars of missed opportunity
There is a shortening of my breath at your shoulder
and the warmth within your sigh encourages tenderness
        This whisper I shall live for generations
You have such wisdom of spirit
It is both naive and erotic

You have no other nature than to be sensual

and I wonder if it is possible
        to want something too much

GRAPPLE FANS

Saturday afternoon she came round unexpected.
All he wanted to do was watch Professional Wrestling
but he knew she expected him to want sex.
It wasn't that he enjoyed watching wrestling, the poor man's Come Dancing
He realised it was all a fake.
He only liked it for the barmy old women ringside.
It was early days in their relationship though and sex was still an
important confirmation of their commitment to each other.
He knew she'd feel rejected if he refused.
He couldn't decide whether it was out of vanity, or more out of insecurity
that he'd been trying to impress her by managing to remain sexually on top
form. Whatever it was, he had thus far set himself a ridiculously high
standard. One he couldn't hope to maintain indefinitely.
Today he didn't feel up to a full performance.
He'd not had a bath in days
and he was wearing those underpants that he always left to the very end of
his clean clothes cycle. The ones with the slogan across the front, '100%
pure beef'.
Not only that, he'd worn them for 2 days now and she'd only ever seen him
in clean underwear before.
Besides he didn't feel romantic.
The atmosphere just wasn't right, the mood wasn't set.
On the TV, stretched out under the bottom rope, a big bloke in a black mask
was being hit over the head with a solid handbag.
'we never talk anymore', he said finally.
Reluctantly she put away her handbag.
Turning down the TV, he pulled off his mask.

LUST AT FIRST SIGHT

Innuendo

connotations

passion plays

mild flirtations

intimate

close relations

breaking down

the reservations

overtures

then separation

regain your pose

polite conversation

averting eyes

no complications

love ? sex ?

or masturbation ?

PASTIMES

We pass the time between orgasms
with reassurance and affection
exploring the contours
drinking the perfume
attentive

We pass the time between orgasms
with cups of coffee
short naps
toast, and maybe the crossword

We pass the time between orgasms
with days apart
work, sleep, routine

We pass the time between orgasms
with hobbies
and interests
escapes
and pastimes

DOES INFLATION AFFECT THE EMOTIONS

Naked as a first kiss, life can be so matter of fact
The attention span of a silverfish, pass the mustard gas

Teenage true love romance
Tongue tied at the wrists
Stood indecisive in your underpants
Grinning like a Christmas guest
Fashion and the smell of sweat
Passion knows no etiquette

Serve me something light, translated from the grief
Pizzaland and the Spud-U-Like, are giving me fatigues

Wake up and smell the coffin
Where do heroes fit the nation
With all the ambition of a homing pigeon
You tune in turn on and flick through the stations
Name dropping at the wishing well
Purple scarred by loose shrapnel

You say 'you don't just stop loving someone', but what if you do ?
You can't beat someone into loving you

Your political leaning's a curvature
With the compassion of a bus inspector
Like your foam filled furniture
Sold in the sale with a smoke detector
Blue murder and Mother's Pride
Don your girdle buckle and hide

Sex becomes the sincerest poetry, the languish of lovers
Time becomes anarchist and Gestapo joins the Marx Brothers

Don't tourist love like a theme park
Turn over the stalls in your temple
Spice racks in the bottom drawer
Of all the lonely lost and hidden people
Now it's user friendly relationships
Not what should be but just what is

Show me more than flesh and fancy, show me something new
Show me love that I may recognise it should it ever enter the room

There's a Phantom at your Opera
There's no such thing as a free verse
Someone's throwing tea into your harbour
And I'm rowing a boat to your Dunkirk
I'll be the last to die at your Alamo
It seems like everyday I'm letting you go

I will always always love only you
Brer Fox, Brer Fox, don't throw me into another love affair
whatever you do

UNDRESSING FOR SEX WHEN YOU FEEL YOU'RE GETTING FAT

It's easy to tell if someone's self-conscious about being overweight
because when they undress for sex
they always take their trousers off
before their shirt.

Another dead giveaway
is the futile attempt to hold their stomach in
whilst trying to pull off their socks.

With practise what usually happens is this -
firstly they make a bee-line for the side of the bed away from the bedside
lamp. Then back turned to both the light and their partner
they slip down their trousers passed their knees
whilst at the same time lowering themselves into the upright sitting
position on the edge of the bed.
Next, they step out of the trouser legs, tread off their socks, undo all
their shirt buttons, breath in and try in one swift movement
to discard their shirt and slip gracefully under the cover.

A complete waste of effort.
No-one, but no-one has a hope in Hell of ever enjoying sex whilst trying to
hold their breath.

Nevertheless, in the cold light of morning
they attempt once more to continue the deception and try desperately
to ooze out of bed un-noticed.

A FISTFUL OF LOVE

Respect and love
go hand in glove
Without love, respect grows cold
Without respect, love becomes
          just an empty covering

FEELING BY NUMBERS

Feeling by numbers
colouring the spaces

joining the dots
filling the blanks

action replacing emotion
like love by committee

discussing the next meeting

reviewing the minutes

the emotion is passed by
show of hands

LEARNING TO UNDERSTAND THE MECHANICS OF THE ECLIPSE

Only the youngest of women left their scent
and friends thought this an inadequacy
Whilst to Nick, as he would have you believe
it was between himself and God alone
Licking the thighs of other women
in the naked sighs of other women, Nick blurred into
all humanity
In the abstract of all masculinity
In the reverence of all femininity
In the perfume of their intimacy, he sought forgiveness
In the schedules of other women he sipped tea
In the flurry of sweat and breath he fought to contain the clouds
Whether he tripped, or was pushed, or whether he jumped
he glimpsed weakness, once and forever weakness
Pressed to the nipple of other women
he crowded his floors
with the tissue bodies of liquid promises
and the scattered mourning clothes of bloodrush and desire
Until
between the devil and the deep blue eyes
grief like a panther fell on him, but here now
curled up in his arms, the crying wound of another's penance
Nick had become a bit player in another's nostalgia
Between empty sheets token gifts winced at the coldness of dead flesh
Here, the softest of mirrors and
now, time to discover, just how pure the bottom line
just how myopic the personification of love
just how selfish melancholy

THE TRAINSPOTTER OF LOVE

She was sophistication personified
an angel with hazel eyes
unmoved by my yearning
to my passion burning
      her indifference would not yield
has the train stopped
my hopes dropped
      and she got off at Macclesfield

A SORT OF MODERN CINDERELLA

Her pen she laid next to mine
round at my pad
then she ran out this morning
without a line
as indeed her pen had

THE MOON DECLARES NOT ITS AGE BUT ITS BEAUTY

Though beurocrats
schedule scorn within their petty margins
and though tomorrow
seems as distant
as the furthest of God's silhouettes

Giddy
to the moment shared
Time is a child running rings in a garden
and the Moon declares not its age but its beauty

Had she have known you then
she would have held you as an infant
in her arms
but
tonight
you hold her in the openness of your kiss

There is a tide within your temples
you
do not look away easily
your face lingers full
your gaze glowing and proud

And for once
    at the foot of the facade
She feels no fear to discard all shadows and excuses

For tonight
the truth of nature will break all regulation
as flowers draw to sunlight through the hardest of concrete.

WILLIAM AND MARY

Mary wore her monogamy like
a thermal vest
She found identity only in coupling
Felt happiness only by proxy
When he left
she lay discarded like a single glove
Self-conscious like a birthday guest
arriving without a present
reduced to reading spines on the bookshelf and
eating savoury Twiglets
Feeling about as useful
as a solitary Argyle sock

LIFE DOWN THE WRONG END OF A TELESCOPE

Is it enough to survive ?
to exist though not feel alive ?
I crave understanding
but feel like the stand-in
for the pilot of Thunderbird 5

YOUR FAVOURITE MUG

Foolish I know
but I feel protective towards your favourite mug
I leave it around the house
as though you were still between sips
as if your lips were just out of the room a moment
and would soon enter and caress its brim
Alone at dusk
I hold it gently, feel its warmth
and drink you in once more

WHEN THE TIME HAS COME TO LEAVE

You can always tell when the time has come to leave
your things start to get put away in cupboards and drawers
out of sight.
Conversations quieten.
People are busy when you enter a room.
Nobody looks you in the face or
asks how you are.

IN THE OPEN CHURCH OF MOUNTAINS LIKE 12 ANGRY JURERS

Hypnotized by oncoming headlights
the idiot beguiled
with humour as bleak as a highland loch
mocked with accommodating smiles
Still looking for love as hardy as bluebells
betrayal's quite funny really
We hide emotions behind glass
never seeing too clearly
Infatuation's a sight common enough
a love-lost caricature
just another walk on part
with delusions of grandeur
who would kiss your blood
and believe it pure
who would kiss your blood and believe it pure
Eternal promises are for all fools day
comically cruel
so mist now softens the skyline
whilst I band aid the ridicule
In the open church of mountains like 12 angry jurors
I serve my solitude,
I feel no guilt, though I know I shouldn't -
I miss you

BREAKING UP IS ...

Breaking up is ...
making a conscious effort to say 'I' instead of 'we'
taking your number down from beside the phone
trying to play only records you never liked
pretending to be busy
trying to think of people worse off
mutual friends being diplomatic, saying 'at least you're both still young'
and 'at least you've got your health'
and other sentences all starting with 'at least'
planning the weekend around half a dozen eggs
not knowing what to do with hands when walking down the street
finding people who look like you attractive
forgiving you everything then nothing every other minute
discounting years in seconds
wanting to talk but wishing too much hadn't been said already

JUNG FREUD AND SINGLE

No more talk
No more reasoning, no more psychoanalysis
Numb like a museum out of season
tonight I just want to get pissed
I thought our love was a bonfire
now it seems we were just burning rubbish

With the dissection of motives
we have driven out innocence
Indulged in wordgames for temporary gain
in some balance sheet romance
Pinned love to the laboratory floor
Bought it whole like a package tour

No more talk of a love with 'ifs and buts'
or of emotions that butter no bread
No more talk of love like a night class
with December on every breath
No more talk of a balance of commitments
or passion being not enough
Love can't be solved like an anagram
yes, maybe I expect too much
In the end there is only faith in one another
In the end there can only be faith

THE NIGHT MY HEART CAUGHT FIRE

The blue lights flashed like a cheap disco at a wedding
6 firemen in yellow hats and matching trousers
jumped out of the red engine and the hoses pissed forth.
As damp rapidly became an understatement
                 a white hat took charge.
'That's the worse case of heartburn I've ever seen' he joked
dragging me unconscious from the wreckage. When eventually I came to I
checked my inside pockets - I was in luck, they'd not wet my matches.

OTHER BOOKS BY HENRY NORMAL NOW IN PRINT -

From:

           A TWIST IN THE TALE PUBLICATIONS
           18 HIND ST. RETFORD, NOTTS. DN22 7EN

Is Love Science Fiction? -
           A5 booklet, 40 pages, glossy cover, bound.
           Update of first collection of Love poems.
           Price £2.30 (inc. p&p)

Love Like Hell -
           A5 booklet, 40 pages, glossy cover, bound.
           Second collection of Love poems.
           Price £2.30 (inc. p&p)

Does inflation affect the emotions? -
           A5 booklet, 40 pages, glossy cover, bound.
           Third collection of Love poems.
           Price £2.30 (inc. p&p)

The Outer Limits of Henry Normal -
           A5 booklet, 36 pages, glossy cover, bound.
           Short comic stories, illustrated.
           Price £3.30 (inc. p&p)